player's) to a vacant space beyond. Blue Frogs can leap likewise, but must leap over 2 counters. If no vacant spaces for Frogs to go to, they may perch on any counter 1 space ahead. Any number of Frogs may be added to the pile, but only the lowest (Frog or Toad) takes its full move or leap; others can move, but only 1 space on (vacant or not). Crossings to the other side by Frogs or Toads must be made on a diagonal slanting back towards an *arrow* and can only involve a move of 1 space.

devised
adapted
and illustrated
by
JOHN ASTROP

KESTREL BOOKS

ROBOTS

Each player has 4 counters; 1 dice.

Object: To get 4 counters round the track from *orange* square to *orange* square.

To Play: Players start from different *orange* squares and move in opposite directions. Take turns to throw dice. You may pass over counters, but if your throw lands your counter on another counter (your

own or your opponent's) you must count your move backwards from where you were when you threw the dice. Landing on any *arrow*, except the 4 centre *crossroads* arrow, moves your counter on a further 2 squares. If you land exactly on a *crossroads* arrow, change tracks, unless a counter (your own or your opponent's) is at the other end. If there is a counter at the other end, move backwards from where you were when you threw the dice.

TOURNE CASE (an old French game)
Each player has 3 counters; 2 dice.
Object: To be first to get all 3 counters from the right-hand side across to the striped panels (*Home*).
To Play: Throw the dice and move forward either 1 or 2 counters (e.g., with a throw of 3, 4, you may either move 1 counter on 7 places or 2 counters on, the one by 3 and the other by 4). Doublets count as a single

(e.g., 5, 5 = 5 only) and only 1 counter can be moved. Counters must remain in their order of entry (the second played cannot pass the first played, etc.), so a counter cannot move if a dice throw would take it on to or beyond one played earlier by the same player. A counter landing on a space directly opposite an opponent's counter sends the opponent's counter back to begin again.

GREEDY BOYS

Each player has 1 counter; 1 dice; a pile of beans, beads or suchlike is used as Store.

Object: To have collected the most pieces of Store when both players have moved off the board. The winner is the Greediest Boy.

To Play: Starting from opposite ends of the board, take turns to move counters, according to dice throw, from square *1* to *25*, through *Feeling*

ill and on again to 1 (opponent's starting place). When you land on a *food* square, take 1 piece from Store. If your opponent is on a *food* square when you land on one, take the piece from his pile. If you land on the same kind of *food* as your opponent is on, take 2 pieces from his pile (but if he has only 1, take the other from Store). If you land on the *Feeling ill* square, you must return all your pieces to Store.

THE LAW OF THE JUNGLE

Each player has 8 counters (marked **1** to **8**) placed on the appropriate animal squares on his side of the board.

Object: To be first to get 1 counter into the enemy's *den*.

To Play: Counters move 1 square up, down or sideways (not diagonally). An animal can kill an animal of an equal or lesser number by landing on its square. The only exception is Rat (**1**), which can kill Elephant (**8**).

(Remove victims from the board.) When Lion (**7**) or Tiger (**6**) reaches any square bordering *water*, it can, next move, leap across *water* to the nearest land square directly opposite. Rat can enter *water* and be safe – no other animal can go in *water* – but it cannot attack Elephant from *water*. A Lion or Tiger cannot jump if Rat blocks way. When an animal lands on *trap* (pink square) on the enemy's side, it can be killed by smaller animal and cannot kill. An animal may not go in its own *den*.

VICIOUS CIRCLES
Each player has 4 counters; 1 dice.
Object: To be first to get all 4 counters from the square on the left to the square on the right.

To Play: Throw 1 to start and throw again for a first move. You can move clockwise or anti-clockwise round the sections of a circle. When you land on a red section, you must follow the arrow into the next circle, whether this takes you onwards or backwards. If you land on another counter (your own or your opponent's) you may move that counter to any unoccupied section of the same colour.

TIGER

One player has 3 counters (Tigers); the other has 15 counters (Lambs).
Object: For Lambs, to block Tigers so that they cannot move; for Tigers, to devour so many Lambs that those remaining are not enough to block them.
To Start: Place Tigers on the 3 blue spots.
To Play: Take turns. Lambs player begins, placing 1 Lamb each turn on any vacant spot (blue or pink). In a turn 1 Tiger can move along any line

to an adjacent vacant spot. If an adjacent spot is occupied by a Lamb, Tiger can devour it by leaping over it to the vacant spot beyond it. (Leaps must be along a straight line, not round a corner.) Victim Lamb is taken off the board and not played again. Lambs are only allowed to move when all of them have been placed. Then they must move along a line to an adjacent vacant spot.

FIFTEEN

Each player has 1 counter; 3 dice (or 1 dice thrown 3 times).

Object: To be first to travel from *1* to *15* and back again to *1*.

To Play: First player throws 3 dice and must try to move square by square, first to *1*, then on to *2, 3, 4* . . . and so on to *15*. The numbers can be used separately (e.g. if player throws 1, 2, 3, he can move to *1*, then on to *2* and on again to *3*, and then throw again). Numbers can also be

added together (e.g., with a throw of 1, 2, 3, you could move to *5* or *6*). But a number on a dice can only be used once in a particular throw (e.g., with a throw of 1, 2, 3, you cannot move to *5* and then on to *6*, because you have used up the 2 and 3 to make 5, so you only have a 1 left). Each player's turn lasts as long as he can throw the next number he requires. When you reach *15*, start back again to finish at *1*.

RAT RACE
Each player has 1 counter; 1 dice.
Object: To be the first rat to get to the *Cheese*.
To Play: Take turns to throw the dice and move forward around the spiral towards the *Cheese.* If your dice throw lands you on a yellow *rest*

square, stop there. If you land on a *trap* square, stop there and miss your next turn. If you land on a rat of another colour, move to the square to which the rat's nose is pointing and go on following the rats' noses until you reach a yellow *rest* square or a *trap* square. All moves from *rest* and *trap* squares continue on round the spiral towards the *Cheese*.

HNEFATAFL (a Viking game)
One player has 1 green counter (the King) and 8 blue counters (the King's Men). The other player has 16 red counters (the Enemy).
Object: For the King's force, to move the King on to one of the 4 corner squares; for the Enemy, to trap the King
To Play: The King is placed in the centre of the board, surrounded by his 8 Men. The Enemy are placed on the 4 lots of 4 squares marked at the

sides of the board. All moves are made 1 square at a time, up or down or sideways (never diagonally). The King's force has first move. A player captures his opponent's counter by trapping it between 2 of his own counters (again, not diagonally). The captured counter is removed from the board. The King is captured only when he is surrounded on all 4 sides.

DOGS AND RABBIT
One player has 4 counters (Dogs) and 2 dice; the other has 1 counter (Rabbit) and uses 1 dice only.
Object: For Dogs, to trap Rabbit so that it is unable to move its next dice throw; for Rabbit, to escape by one of the 4 path openings at the edge of the board.
To Play: Place 1 Dog at each of the 4 path openings. Place Rabbit on 1 of the large black spots (*rabbit holes*). Dogs and Rabbit move along red

and black spots in any direction. Dogs player throws first and can move any combination of 1, 2, 3 or 4 Dogs the total score of 2 dice (throw of 5, 3 moves each Dog 2 spots on, or 1 Dog 8 spots on, etc.). Rabbit, when on a *rabbit hole,* may, before dice throw, burrow directly to next vacant *rabbit hole* along the path. It may pass under Dogs when burrowing directly, but neither Rabbit nor Dogs may pass each other on a dice throw.

SCRUMPING

One player has 1 green counter, the other has 1 blue counter; 4 red and 4 yellow counters (Fruit) are placed in the tree; 2 dice.

Object: To be first to collect 4 Fruits in a *basket*.

To Play: Take turns to throw 2 dice and subtract the lesser number from the greater one. For example, a throw of 6, 4 moves a counter 2 places (6 − 4 = 2). You can move your own counter or your opponent's, either

up or down. Doublets (6, 6; 5, 5, etc.) miss a turn. When your counter lands exactly on a top square, place 1 Fruit on top of it and try to get the Fruit down. When you land exactly on the bottom square, you can put the Fruit safely in your *basket*. If you land on the square next to your opponent's counter when it is loaded with a Fruit, your counter captures that Fruit (or Fruits) and you have another throw.

MU TORERE (a Maori game)
Each player has 4 counters.
Object: To block your opponent's counters so that they cannot move.
To Play: The counters of one player are placed on the blue points and those of the other player are placed on the green points. The point at the centre is called the *Putahi*. Only 1 counter may occupy any of the outer points or the *Putahi* at any time. Take turns to move any 1 of your counters. A counter may be moved: (a) directly to an adjacent point; (b) from an outer point to the *Putahi*, provided that 1 or both adjacent points are occupied by a counter belonging to your opponent; (c) from the *Putahi* to any unoccupied point.

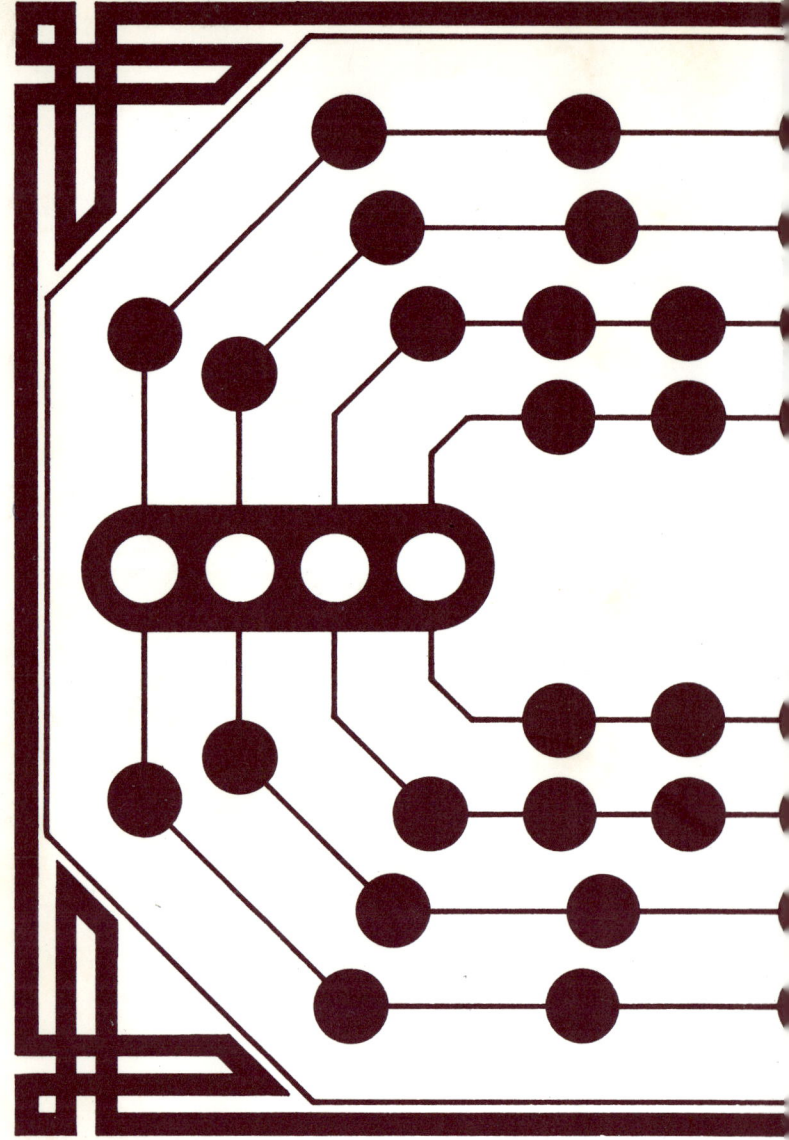

SPOOF

4 counters are shared by both players.

Object: To force your opponent to make the last move, which is the removal of the last counter from the board.

To Play: Place the counters on the 4 spots enclosed within the bar (*Home*). Take turns to move any counter clockwise around the spots on